I curl
beneath
the covers.

pull my knees
to my chest.

and whisper
to
myself.

"every inch of you
is loved."

I dunk
my head
into the tub.

watch
as the dye and my hair
ripple
out.

and
separate.

I watch
as the water
returns me.

the water returns
me.

heavy.

the universe
knows.

two men
were shot

on my block
this week.

1 killed.

walking home
it's hard

not to remember

how quickly
things can
end.

heavy.




you live here
long enough

and you learn.

guns fire
from the quiet corners
too.

I look at you
and want

to unfold you.

lay you out
like a map.

trace your continents
with my finger.

circle it
somewhere
around your center.

point to it
and say,
there.

see I promised you.

it's always been
right

there.

heavy.

it is the last truly hot day
of summer

and I
am wearing
a sweater.

when I feel
it.

I want to really
feel

it.

today
I order
the shrimp and grits.

I can't exactly afford.

I eat them naked.
and alone.

I let the red sauce
drip

down
my fingers.

teeth
fighting
knuckles.

I lick it
off.

heavy.

this is
the someday.

you've been waiting
for.

you carved
a place
for
yourself

in my heart.

and now it feels
like

something is missing.

while
you're gone.

heavy.

forget the notion
that
you can't heal.

at the very least
I know
you can cope.

it is what you're doing now
even while
you're reading this.

you tell me
you like

my intensity.
call yourself
a moth

to my flame.
its cheesy, but I love you anyway.

and then you love me.
too much
you say.

say
I make you feel
like
a shadow.

like
a ghost
of yourself.

you say if I loved you.
wanted you.

to be
everything.
you could be.

to me.

I would simmer down.
and burn.

just a little less.

heavy.

I won't apologize
for being
too

much

when you have refused

to be
enough.

I love your
hairy
butt

and the way
your lips crack

when you smile.

I wish I could show
you

how
deeply
I admire

the most tender
and untamed
regions
of
you.

heavy.

I'm afraid

when I make it
to
bed.

of how badly

I will want
you.

beside me.

write
like it's a funeral.

write
like it's an execution.

write
like everything you ever wanted came true and you
rotted anyway.

write
like you're gutting the poison out.

pull your heart back into yourself.
take deep breathes.
heal.

heavy.

write
like it's your last chance
at hope.
and happiness.
and forgiveness.
and trust.

write
like you're explaining your heart.

to yourself.

because
you are.

and it will save you.

what is it like
to be
woman?

I am filled
to the brim
with anger.

I am filled
to the brim
with care.

heavy.

you say,
"there will be consequences."

like
I don't know.

like I haven't
always

known.

you speak.

over
me.

and I think
I cannot love you.

I have practiced
my voice.
too long.

not
to be heard.

heavy.

you will know
when
you meet them.

they will
be

bringing you
the peace.

you need
to understand.

if you are going to love me.

you can't be afraid.

of the
way
I will love you

back.

like the earth
cracking
open,
to swallow
you
whole.

because letting
you feast
on me

just
isn't enough.

I just want all of you
too.

heavy.

I don't want you
to move
mountains.

I just want
you

to sit down.
and love me.

you said,
I don't know how
to fix
you.

I said,
you

aren't supposed to.

heavy.

I said,
"I'm happy with my life right now."

you said,
"I think it's nice that you're trying
to be."

sometimes
I think

you
don't know

you
are the poison.

you look me in the eye
and grin.

as her hands
trace
the familiar terrain
of your chest.

you do not understand.

I will not fight
for what
doesn't want me.

I will evacuate

to the safe
spaces
that ask
me to stay.

heavy.


I get it
you love
the misery.

and you see
sometimes
it lives
in me.

but I'm going to have
to ask

you to stop feeding
the things

I'm trying
to kill.

you think I don't know
the difference

between looking
and

sizing up the weak.

heavy.

writing
is just like boxing

without gloves.

you didn't know me.

just
the smell
of my skin.

heavy.

how to unlearn

bartering
forgiveness.

I look down at the hot blood
spreading

between the legs
of my jeans

and smile
at my own body's
rebellion.

not just woman
when it's convenient.

not just here
when you want me.

heavy.

but
you don't have to bleed
to be.

I press
my open mouth
against your skin.

taste
the salt
of your flesh
across my tongue.

I know
this isn't what you meant.

but does it still count?

as letting you in?

heavy.

we drove to a new state today.
I sat in a new city.

saw piles of people
I thought
all looked the same.

this morning
things were fine.
and now I've
gone
and opened my mouth.
let slip

all
the feelings.

I've been burying.
all week.

heavy.

purge
then purge
and purge.

until you feel
that brain
clean.

I remember
when the months
didn't sound so fragile.

before.

I knew
it's name.

heavy.

I still don't regret
it.

remember
when you met them.

the ones with gravestones
for eyes.

it doesn't have
to be
your
business.

what ever they keep
buried

there.

heavy.

you
have a kind
face.

and a strong
back.

but that still
doesn't make them
your burden

to carry.

I am in a room
I imagined

when I was fourteen.

tangled
in bed

with a 6ft
barrel chested
version

of my dreams.

heavy.

you knew
all the ways

to bring

the softness
back

to me.

I've been grabbing thorns
all morning

trying
to decide

which of them
I need to.

heavy.

will you bring

the
silence?

spent the afternoon
chasing sunlight
across my bed

as it shifted
from my shoulder
to my knee.

trying
to forget.

the darkness still
comes.

heavy.

my clothes are still sticking
to my skin.
but the sun leaves
me

too
early.

this
time
when
everything feels

like too much.

and
still
not
enough.

you spill
a list

of ways
to soothe

the hurt
between my body

and
self.

but you point to my parts
and use the word
fix

and your words
dig a trench
where I needed
a bridge.

heavy.

I tried
what you said.

to be better.
but found

I was happier

when I settled
for being myself
instead.

I press my lips
gently

against
the palms

of
your hands.

I know.
what you've done.

heavy.

every morning
I just iron out
my heart.

and
wait.

for it to come.

tonight
I almost gave up
the writing
the solitude
and the gin.

what is the immortality of words
next to your soft
skin?

heavy.

what you need
when you need it

most.

tonight

we drank wine
ate sushi
made love
and too many jokes.

in a room
on the 22nd floor
of a hotel

right around the corner
from

who
we used to be.

heavy.

if I could write
you

a love song
it would just be
the sound

of
our laughter

harmonizing

in a loop.
on repeat.

scars
aren't proof

that you didn't heal.

just that
you
changed.

faster than you might have.

heavy.

but
you are still
a body.

how do you take

all
of that?

I practice
cleaning

my home
as if

it were my
heart.

I get behind the furniture
into all the corners
directly through
the messes
I so carefully avoid.

I'm doing my best
to practice

drudging
the dirt
out.

heavy.

I didn't know
the
difference

between your and you're
until

my college roommate
told me

only idiots
don't know.

and
this has all been a lesson

in never
underestimating
a person's

ability
to learn.

it's
not your fault

you
couldn't teach

what
you didn't know.

heavy.

you make
a small kindness
and I tuck it away

for safe keeping.

that is how
I love you.

20 times a day
I fight back the urge
to tell you.

you are the most beautiful
soul.

and I think that heart of yours
could heal cities
back whole.

heavy.

my sadness
isn't the absence
of joy.

it is learning.
how

to trace
a habit

down to its root
and pull.

it wasn't a quick process.
you leaving.

it was waking up
every day
for months

and feeling you
beside me

just a little
less.

heavy.

sometimes
I just want to pretend
to
be weak.

I just want to forget.

I had to learn
so early.

how to be
enough.

the hardest part
isn't
leaving.

it is
in
 the staying.

even
after

there is nothing
left

to
prove.

heavy.

I walk into
our
room

and you don't demand
the words
from me.

you just
open

your arms
and
give.

"you date an awful lot of people."

"sometimes
salvation comes
with a lot of faces."

heavy.

most people
don't seem to know

acknowledgement

is fucking
required.

I am
broke
and eating eggs
everyday

but I spent
an afternoon
and
twenty dollars
on drinks

and
forgetting

your name.

it was
worth
more.

heavy.




a hand or a diamond.

works just the same.

it all comes.
it all leaves.

you are
your own.

heavy.

I know,
I keep telling you

but

repetition
is

key.

my ankles
are my favorite
part

of my body
even if

they are easiest
to break.

heavy.

but what is
breaking

when it teaches
you

to heal.

I pull and comb the hair slick
to my skull.

tie it back tight.
watching the mirror.

undress and pose.
with the gut
dimples
and lips
hanging
loose.

I frown and  I scowl and I moan.
I practice making
ugly.
to remind myself

love
doesn't come

from
the outside
in.

heavy.




you
are ready
to know

yourself.

just hold your heart steady

and
listen.

sometimes
I wish

I could draw you
an understanding

of my
heart.

because sometimes even
good words
lose

meaning.

heavy.

you love the fall
and
setting suns

and I feel wary
to love
anyone

so in love
with endings.

I have built myself
into
the strongest
structure.

sometimes
it's hard
to appreciate
added support

as more
than wasted
effort.

heavy.

I am
trying

to
unlearn

alone.

you taught me
how to be patient.
how to be too
kind.

how to translate
your knife
in my gut

to
I love you.

when you should have taught me
how and when
to run.

heavy.


I spend the night
on the edge

of
the bath

lathered up
and working
through

my
limbs.

running water
for warmth.

hands cupping
and pouring.

the heat
over
me.

I bring myself
to softness.

I let myself be
the
honey.

you pull me
in with those big arms.

my panicked heart
slows.

finds its pace
in time.
with yours.

and
that is
how

I know.

heavy.

give yourself
the time

you
need.

you've brought poison
into my home.
too many times
this week.

you can learn
how to
suck

your own venom
out.

heavy.

I'm listening to music
that doesn't know

it's own name.

and pretending
I don't know

my own.

I see you
too far away
to talk.

still close enough
to touch.

at the bar
and it is dark
and red lit
and closed.

the jazz wraps
itself

around
me

as I
wrap
myself

around
you.

it could have been
anyone

but here we are
and
it's us.

heavy.

you are
a different

sun.

but we
share

the most tender
moon.

people say
that it was complicated.

but all it really took
was two people

with faith

in
each other.

heavy.


there is always
that one

you turn
and open
to.

you think
it is destiny.

in a way

it is.

I wish
you'd stop
telling me

about
all the freak
accidents

you read
about
and watched

on
the internet.

it's hard enough
not to focus
on all the regular
things

that go wrong.

much less
all of these improbable
extras.

heavy.

you finish the whiskey
and press fingertips
against your eyes.

"I think I'm going off the deep end."

I laugh
and cup
your cheeks
with my hands.

"I can teach you
how to float."

gin with bitters,
soda water and lime.

whiskey with honey,
lemon and ice.

tequila with salt,
a wedge and your skin.

how do you
always know.

how
to wash

the acid
out.

heavy.

you kiss
where my shoulder
meets
my neck.

and I realize
how very wrong

I
have been.

I imagine the way
things
will look

when things
are
different.

it looks like a room
with
windows.

and morning
light.

too many plants.
and no
one

to tell me

how
to be

where I belong.

heavy.

why

did you let yourself
do that?

why

are you still?

here I am
just doing

all
the things.

I promised you
I wouldn't.

heavy.


my hair
grows
wilder

in your hands.

and your lips
remind me

I never was one to stay

quiet.

grey skies
and the sound
of rain.

chili
on the stove
and you
naked

in my tub.

there are no words
good enough

for that.

heavy.

cover
my mouth

when I ask you.

protect me.

from
myself.

where
will it all come from?

and
how

will it stay?

heavy.

few phrases
more dangerous
than

this time
last year.

in my head
she spreads
her legs

for the same
hands
that forced
their way between
mine.

and I feel
sick
and jealous

that she got a choice
to be willing.

heavy.

december 21
is the darkest
day

of the year.

for me
it is my favorite.

it is when
things begin
to
get light.

love isn't something
you fight
for.

it is something
you learn

how
to get gentle
and give.

heavy.

it's hard
to remember

what safety was
before

your heavy arm
pressing

over
my chest

and

the sound
of your breathe

beside
me.

the moon is lacing
itself

through
my curtains.

dancing
across

my skin.

my blood is waiting.

I already
feel

the fullness.

of
the night.

heavy.

my skin
is on fire.

and you

keep me begging.

for
water.

the sweat is heavy.
and pungent.
and unapologetic.

it reeks of long walks
sex
and the summer
days.

it reminds me of those times
my body
and I

were so happy
together.


to be alive.

heavy.

you keep trying
to teach me

I'm the wrong kind
of kindness.

but I still
don't
believe

there is a bad way.
to be good.

it's not
your body's
fault.

heavy.

you were worth

the
forgiveness.

sometimes
the intensity

of a good
thing

is still too much.

to
handle.

heavy.

I'm just
waiting

for a moment

to
melt.

in your hands.

sometimes.

loving me
is understanding.

the way fires  start
with even
the most loving
and
gentle
of brushes
against my skin.

I am half
match stick
part
kerosene.

heavy.

all
it takes

is a slip

of a
trigger.

you told me
about bringing joy

to
yourself.

in the bathroom cabin
of a plane.

flushed cheeks.
sticky skin.
a mouth
without apologies.

and you reminded
me then.

how
to love .


myself.

heavy.

I'm sorry,

but it's hard
to imagine.

loving
you.

any less.

it lands
somewhere
on my shin.

I freeze.
if I flinch
will it hurt me?

you laugh.
you don't understand.

heavy.

I can measure

the difference
between understanding
and
forgiveness

by the arm
lengths

between us.

don't be afraid.
of my anger.

it won't hurt.
you.

be afraid of the men.
and the mouths.
and the hands
and the tongues.
and the force.

that were used.
to plant
rot.

where the sweetness
used to
grow.

heavy.

but I will weed
and harvest
my own gardens.

no remorse
for pulling

what should
never
have been

planted.

I sleep
with a knife
down my spine

the first night
in every
new bed.

that is how
and
when

I
remember

you.

heavy.

tonight
I was in the shower
with another
man.

but it was different.

when I said stop
he listened.

you were the first
time

I thought
I couldn't do this.

you won't
be
the last time.

I was wrong.

heavy.

what I'm trying
to say

is
"I love you."

but
it just keeps
coming out
as

"I'm sorry"
"I'm scared"
and
"you're wrong."

my tongue
hits

the rind.
and sweet juice
rolls

down my chest.

I suck
until
the pink
turns
white.

and there is nothing
left.

heavy.

I sleep with knotted fingers
in your mouth.

tangled hair
around your throat.

boney knees
pressed
between your soft flesh.

but
you say
too close
still isn't close

enough.

we woke again
and it was

storming.

I should have known.

you knew.
it was

coming.

heavy.

I look around
the living room

you say
my life is a mess.

but
the house plants
are
still just growing.

pressing toes
against white ceramic.

knees pulled up
above water.

my hair floats
into
a crown.

I let myself sink.
as
far
as
I'll go.

setting myself up.
to
rise.

again.

heavy.

you are still
where

the good things

grow.

a mouthful of wine
and laughter
leaking

through my teeth.

you are burning sage
in a circle
around my skull.

a hand full of rings.

you say,
"let's pray
for your intentions."

and I think the moon
was made
for us.

heavy.

I pass a man
selling pit bulls in the street
yelling

"good fighters,
I swear!
great deal."

as I walk to the home
of a woman
who saves
them.

how do we
unteach them

this?

how do we save them.

all.

people took
the seats
left
and right

of me.
it was difficult to hide

my disappointment.

you said
"I don't trust women
who wear hats."

I said
"funny,
I don't trust people
who say shit
like that."

you said, "you're a very powerful
person"

and I asked, "why
can't you love me?"

you said, "two positive ions,
they repel."

heavy.

never
out of
spite.

I slice
my foot.

on a shard
of the wine glass
you broke
and
didn't clean
up.

and feels
like you

never
left.

heavy.

it's awful
the way

I can twist
your slightest trespass

into a siege
on my whole city.

you can't tell
the difference

between
my body
and love.

that is why
you
don't touch
me.

that is why
I
don't love
you.

heavy.

you look at me like
continents.

you want to devour.

I learned how to love you
even while

you loved
someone else.

but I learned how to love you.
to keep
my hands to myself.

I learned how to trust.

I learned how to not.
push.

heavy.

you
still cross my mind
every time.
I cross
the street.

and it's been years.
but I still wonder.

would you still
be

breathing

if
I had loved you

enough?

you
were the first.

I had to
leave

behind.

heavy.

when
will my forgiveness
come?

tonight
you made me dinner

and I rubbed oil
through your hair.

we laughed at the same things.
and split
all our beers.

and even if
you leave me.

I promise,
I'll still think

it was a miracle.

you were here.

heavy.

the kindness
is a vine

that grows
from your heart
to mine.

the apartment is hot
and I am alone.
except for the fridge,
that groans
against the silence.

I tip the whiskey
towards me.
ice knocks hard
against
the glass.

is alone the same
as

absolution.

heavy.




you don't understand
the way
I love
the rain.

I think you must
not know.

what it's like.

to feel
unclean.

I hope you warn her.

when she touches
you.

she can use the salt
the vinegar
and sage.

but none of that
will
wash.

the smell of me
on you.

out.

heavy.

you held my head
to
your sweaty
neck.

built me a fortress
of
your limbs.

pressed my heartbeat
against
yours

until
I felt safe.

and lost my grip

on
the fear
and the rage.

and I can't help
but wonder

could loving
have always
been

so
simple?

sometimes you just need
a few weeks

not to wear
you're own
skin.

I won't blame you.
for being who you had to be

then.

heavy.


I know
the hurts are hard

to hear.

but

I'll tell you
of the kindness

too.

some people ask things
like how
or what happened.

but
what they mean is

did you ask for it?


what they mean is
have you been told

for so long

that your significance
only starts
and ends

when men walk in
and out

of your room

that you began to believe it?

heavy.

they mean to ask you,
have we convinced you
that

your body only begins to exist
with his presence in it?

and if you couldn't be loved
did some dead part of you
hope

to be hit.

because if you couldn't be loved
did you settle

just to exist?

sitting at the bar
with you

and laughing
until it rings
out

the windows.

listening
to the music
not watching
as

it rains.

heavy.

blessed are
moments.

you are allowed

to
forget.

I watched you
drink.

until the sadness
left
your smile.

I watched you
drink.

until your heart
left it
too.

heavy.

complicit.

I feel
complicit.

it feels
just like screaming.

without
a
mouth.

heavy.

my blood
is on
your clean sheets.

you slapped my side
and called it

knocking
the rust
out.

I'm sorry.

I came
here

because it's what
I thought

that I wanted.
but

I realize now

it's really
really
not.

heavy.

you asked me
what I really

want.

so I told you.

"when I want
to
shrink,

please,
don't let me."

I walk home
alone
at night

and my face cracks
into a laugh.

this is what
it feels like

not
to hide.

heavy.

it's no ones fault.

I don't think
either of us.

expected
me

to learn
or change
so
quick.

I love to use the word
flesh.

I love to remind
you

that I am more
than

just warmth
and
skin.

that I am
all
the depths

beneath
it
too.

heavy.

I am more

than
just

your
muse.

you said

the weight
of my presence
is even
too heavy.

for you.

you don't like
the
reminders

of what you've never
had

to carry.

heavy.

bodies manage
to bend and
give
and heal

even in ways
they're not supposed
to.

you
can too.

things
are so different
now.

I can't
remember.

who

I used to be.

heavy.

forgiveness, forgiveness, forgiveness.

forgiveness.

forgiveness.

how do I?

forgiveness.

you said my greatest
weakness

is admitting
all
my flaws.

but
I think
I've just learned.

how to bend
here
before

I would have
cracked.

heavy.

this morning

my kitchen
is still a mess.

I might keep it.
a small alter

to remind me.
the good things

don't always
look nice.

 I am wearing a sweater
that smells
like someone
else.

I bought it
at the thrift store.

but I still
feel

less
alone.

heavy.

sometimes you just need
a few weeks

not to wear
you're own
skin.

I won't blame you.
for being who you had to be

then.

no one else
can

save you.

but
the love
you learn

with
them

could.

heavy.

letting go

and
remembering.

this is now.

how
I love you.

I stare at you
across the table
and at

the distance
growing

between us.

you grab my hand
to remind me
how far

we've come.

heavy.

I was weak
and
then I was angry.

I was angry
and so I got sad.

I was sad
and
it made me soft.

I was soft
and then

I found
the strength

in
that.

sit here, quietly,
twist my fingers
into knots.

so very afraid.

all my dreams.
might come true.

what
then?

heavy.

sleep
when you can.

eat the fruit
while it's there.

love
while it is
there.

leave
when it hurts.

heal
with your heart open.

let it rain.

start again.

I remember
when

I used to look
at you
and say

"it is coming."

and now
we sit
quietly

and
it is here.

heavy.

you rarely exit

the same
way

you came.

99516971R00102

Made in the USA
Columbia, SC
10 July 2018